i love crochet

i love crochet

25 PROJECTS THAT WILL SHOW YOU HOW TO CROCHET EASILY AND QUICKLY

RACHEL HENDERSON & SARAH HAZELL

PHOTOGRAPHY BY KATE WHITAKER

KYLE CATHIE LTD

how to crochet

We'll begin this section by saying, don't worry, the key to crochet is persistence, so don't get disheartened after a few attempts. Once you've got a grasp of the basics, it's all about practising how to hold the yarn and perfecting how to move the hook so that you can achieve a good tension. As your confidence starts to grow you can start adding beads and sequins or move onto our decorative stitches. Most of all, have fun and think creatively. Good luck!

choosing a hook & yarn

Holding a crochet hook and yarn is really straightforward. In fact, it really shouldn't take long before it becomes second nature. It's so easy, you'll soon be crocheting on the bus or in the pub with your friends.

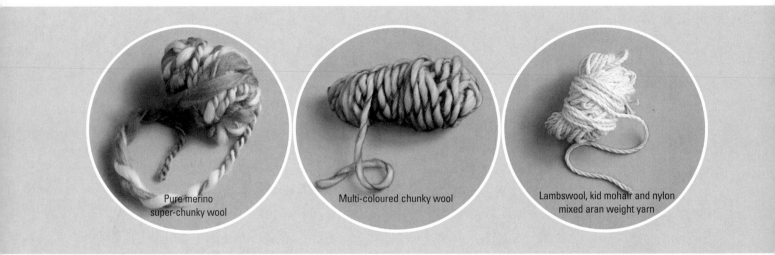

Pure merino
super-chunky wool

Multi-coloured chunky wool

Lambswool, kid mohair and nylon
mixed aran weight yarn

YARNS

There are many different types of yarns on the market. Each type of yarn has a particular weight and composition. Depending on the size of hook you use, they all give a different type of fabric. Crochet makes a thicker and firmer fabric than knitting, so take that into account when choosing your yarn, hook and stitch.

The three factors you should take into account when choosing a yarn are its weight (or thickness), composition (what it's made of) and length.

Weight This is based on the number of plies (or strands) the yarn is made of. The thinnest yarn is 2 ply and it goes up in size through 4 ply, double knit (DK), aran and chunky to super-chunky.

Composition Yarns are made up of different fibres, from natural ones such as merino wool, alpaca, silk, cotton and linen to man-made ones like nylon, acrylic and viscose. The yarn's ball band will tell you what the yarn is made of and give you washing information.

Length The meterage of yarn in a ball can vary, even if the yarns are the same type and the balls weigh the same. It is the meterage that is vital, so if you are using a different yarn to the one in the pattern, check the ball for the meterage and make sure you buy enough for the total length required by the pattern.

HOOKS

Crochet hooks come in different types, shapes and sizes. It's up to you to decide whether you prefer hooks made of aluminium, steel, plastic or bamboo. Steel and aluminium hooks often have a strong plastic middle and end, which is easy to grip and lighter on your fingers. Some hooks have a flat middle, which is also easy to grip. Try out different hooks until you find the one that's most comfortable for you.

The size of hook you use is all-important. A pattern will always recommend which size to use, but it depends on the weight of the yarn and your tension. If you use a big hook with chunky yarn, your crochet will grow quickly, or more slowly if you opt for a smaller hook. Crochet hooks are generally the same length as you only ever have a few loops on the hook at any given time.

If you choose a different yarn from the one sugested, it's important to match the tension to the one given in the pattern. For more information on tension, see page 14.

Softly twisted chunky cotton and acrylic mix

Pure silk double knitting yarn

Double knitting wool and cotton mix

Super kid mohair and silk mixed 4 ply

equipment

All you really need is some yarn and a hook that's comfortable to use. But, as you make more projects, you might like to buy a few more pieces of equipment that will make your life a little easier.

1 Ruler or tape measure This is a handy thing to have, especially when checking your tension square at the beginning of a project.

2 Sewing needles A tapestry needle is used for darning in ends and sewing up your crocheted project. If you are using a very chunky yarn, make sure you choose a needle with an eye large enough to take the yarn. You may also need a finer needle if you wish to incorporate beads in your crochet.

3 Scissors A small pair of scissors is always useful for trimming ends of yarn.

4 Pins When you are sewing up your crocheted project, you will find these helpful for keeping the fabric in place.

5 Notepad and pen Always useful to have on hand, especially if you are designing a new project, or just need to keep count of your rows, rounds and different stitches.

6 Crochet markers These help to identify which row you are on – especially handy when you are working in a round.

tension

The way you hold the yarn and hook will give you a specific tension determining how tight or loose your crocheted fabric is.

Tension is how tightly or loosely you crochet – or the number of stitches and rows in a given crocheted fabric. The tension will affect the size of your finished project. If you crochet more tightly than the pattern recommends, your project will end up too small, and if you crochet more loosely, it might be too big.

Always crochet a tension square before you start a project. Use the same yarn, type of stitch and size of hook as the pattern recommends, and check that your tension matches the pattern.

If you want to use a different yarn, it must also give the same tension. Use the same stitch because each one gives a different height, which will affect the number of rows in a given measurement. If you want to change the type of stitch suggested in a pattern, you will need to calculate how many more or fewer rows make the same length of fabric. The thickness of a crochet hook of the same size can vary slightly, which might affect your tension – so you may need to change to a bigger or a smaller size to get the right tension.

MEASURING YOUR TENSION SQUARE

The pattern will tell you how many stitches and rows you should have in a 10cm/4in square. Crochet a slightly larger square and fasten it off. Place a tape measure horizontally across the square and, starting a few stitches from the edge, position pins 10cm/4ins apart. Count the stitches between the pins.

Then place the tape measure vertically across the square and position pins 10cm/4cm apart. Count the number of rows between the pins.

When working a more decorative stitch pattern, your tension will be measured according to the repeat pattern rather than the number of stitches and rows. In that case, count the number of pattern repeats between the pins.

If you have too few stitches or repeats, try again with a larger hook. If you have too many, use a smaller hook. Don't try to crochet at a different tension to what comes naturally – you won't be able to keep it up throughout the project.

holding your hook & yarn

Holding your crochet hook and yarn can feel awkward at first. But persistence is the key and once it feels right, you're off! Try holding the hook loosely just before you start to work with the yarn, either with an overhand grip or as if you were holding a pen.

HOLDING THE HOOK

Here are the two most common ways of holding the hook in your right hand. Practise both and find the way that feels most comfortable.

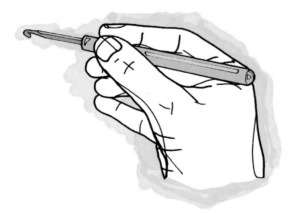

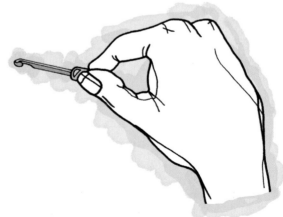

Writing grip Hold the middle of the hook between your thumb and index finger, so that the hooked side is facing you and the rest of it is supported by your hand – just as if you are about to write with it.

Overhand grip Hold the middle of the hook with the tips of your thumb and index finger, so that the hooked side is facing you and your hand is above the hook.

HOLDING THE YARN

With the hook in your right hand, you'll need your left hand to hold your work and the yarn. It's worth getting this right, as the way you hold the yarn controls the tension and keeps it even. Practise both methods to see which way works best for you.

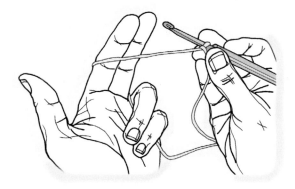

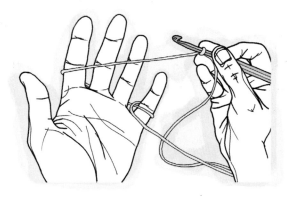

Two-finger grip Take the working end of the yarn (the one attached to the ball) loosely around the back of the index and middle fingers on your left hand. Grip the yarn firmly with your last two fingers against your hand.

One-finger grip Take the working end of the yarn around the back of the first three fingers on your left hand. Bring it in front of your little finger and wrap it right around that finger again. You can tighten your grip on the yarn by pressing your little finger against your ring finger.

HOLDING THE WORK

With the working end of the yarn secure, take tight hold of your work with your left thumb and index finger close to the hook. Don't hold the hook too tight or your tension will be tight.

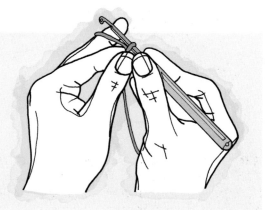

basic techniques

To start any crochet you need a foundation chain. It's just like a cast-on row in knitting and provides the basic foundation for the rest of the crocheted fabric. The number of chains you make determines the width of the fabric.

SLIP KNOT

1 To start a foundation chain, leave a short tail of yarn and make a slip knot by winding the yarn twice around two fingers on your left hand. Hold the loose end of yarn secure with your thumb and take the second loop behind the first one.

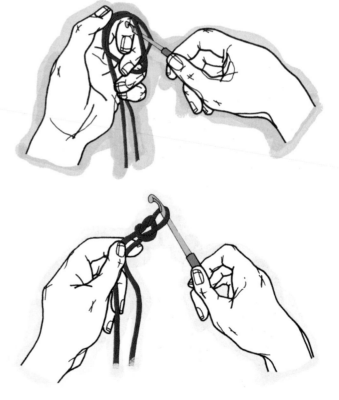

2 Pull the second loop of yarn through the first loop either with the crochet hook or your right-hand fingers.

3 Slip the new loop onto the crochet hook and tighten it up by gently pulling on the loose end of yarn. Remember not to make the slip knot too tight; you can slacken it off again by gently pulling on the working end of the yarn.

MAKING A FOUNDATION CHAIN

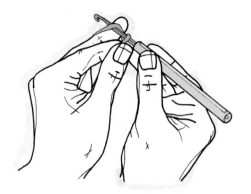

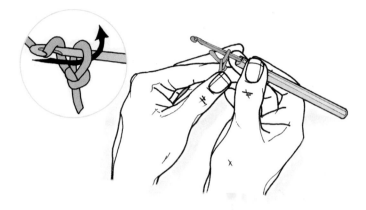

1 Firmly hold the slip knot with your left index finger and thumb. Hold the crochet hook in your right hand. Lifting your left middle finger to tension the yarn, slide the hook over the working yarn from above (this often called 'yarn over' or 'yo') Rotating the hook slightly, secure the yarn under the hook end.

2 Pull the hook back through the slip knot. Repeat this process, continually adjusting your left-hand grip to hold the work near the hook, until the required number of chain stitches has been made.

RACHEL'S & SARAH'S TIP:
When making your foundation chain, make sure the chain stitches aren't too tight, otherwise it can be difficult to get the hook through each chain stitch for your next row.

COUNTING CHAIN STITCHES

Count your chains before you begin the next row, then you'll be sure to make the right width of fabric.

Make sure the foundation chain is not twisted and that the fronts of the chains are facing you. Count the number of loops – each one counts as one chain stitch. When you count, always ignore the initial slip knot and the loop on your hook.

WORKING INTO THE FOUNDATION CHAIN

With the right length of foundation chain, you are ready to work the first row. This can be quite tricky if the foundation chain is tight and it can be hard to see each chain stitch. Here are two ways of working – either will make it easier.

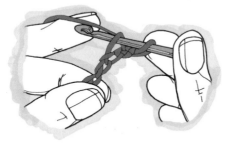

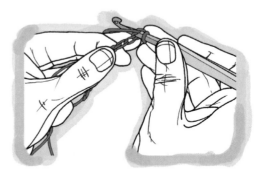

Method 1 Flip the foundation chain over and slide the crochet hook from front to back through the top of the second chain stitch from the hook. Take the working yarn over the hook. Draw the yarn through the foundation chain stitch to make another loop on the hook. Complete the new chain stitch according to the pattern. Make the next stitch into the very next chain on the foundation chain. Continue in this way to the end.

Method 2 If you hold the foundation chain with the fronts of the chain stitches facing you, you can see that they each make a sideways 'v' shape. Slide the crochet hook from front to back under the second 'v' shape from the hook, making sure it goes under two loops. Take the working yarn over the hook and draw it through so there's a loop on the hook. Complete the new stitch according to the pattern. Make the next stitch into the very next 'v' shape on the foundation chain. Continue in this way to the end.

MAKING A TURNING CHAIN

To keep the shape of your crochet even, you need to make one or more turning chains at the beginning of each row. These are simple chain stitches and the number you need depends on the type of stitch in the next row. The number of stitches you need in your turning chain to match various stitches are given are as follows:

Double crochet: 1 turning chain.
Half treble crochet: 2 turning chains.
Treble crochet: 3 turning chains.
Double treble crochet: 4 turning chains.

When you work most stitches, count the turning chain as the first stitch. However, when you are working double crochet, ignore the turning chain – it doesn't count it as a stitch.

basic stitches

Here are a few stitches you can work into the foundation chain. They are all worked in the same basic way, but the differences are achieved by changing the number of times you wind the yarn around the hook and the number of loops you pull the hook through.

SLIP STITCH (ss)

This is used to sew up crocheted fabrics and to complete a round.

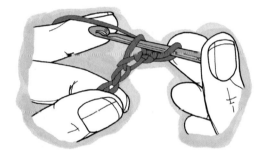

① Slide the hook through the last chain stitch worked on the foundation chain, to give two loops on the hook. Take the working yarn over the hook.

② Draw the hook, and yarn, back through both loops on the hook. Slide the hook through the next chain stitch on the foundation chain and repeat the process to the end of the row.

WORKING IN ROWS

Always work from right to left along the rows. When you come to the end of a row you will need to turn your work. It doesn't matter whether you turn it clockwise or anti-clockwise – as long as you turn it the same way every time, the fabric will stay flat.

Your yarn should always be sitting at the back of your work before you make your chain stitches at the beginning of a new row. This will enable you to maintain a straight and neat edge.

DOUBLE CROCHET (dc)

This is one of the simplest, and most commonly used, crochet stitches.

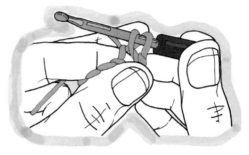

① At the beginning of the row, first add one extra chain stitch to make the turning chain. Then slide the hook into the second chain stitch on the foundation chain.

② Take the working yarn over the hook and pull the yarn back through the first loop on the hook. Take the yarn over again and pull it back through both loops to give just one new loop on the hook. Repeat steps 1 to 2 to the end of the row, working into the next chain stitch on the foundation chain.

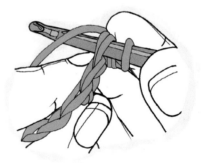

③ At the end of the row, turn your work and make one turning chain. On all rows after the first one, make double crochets in the same way as in steps 1 and 2, but sliding the hook under both loops at the top of each stitch (the 'v' shape described on page 20).

TREBLE CROCHET (tr)

Treble crochet produces an open fabric, because the yarn is wound around the hook three times to create long stitches.

1 At the beginning of the row, first add a turning chain of three extra stitches. Take the working yarn over the hook. Then slide the hook into the fourth chain from the hook on the foundation chain.

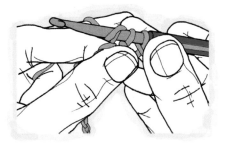

2 Take the yarn over the hook and pull it back through the first loop on the hook. You should now have three loops on the hook again.

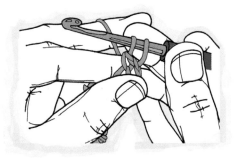

3 Take the yarn over the hook and pull it back through the first two loops on the hook. You will now have two loops on the hook. ➤

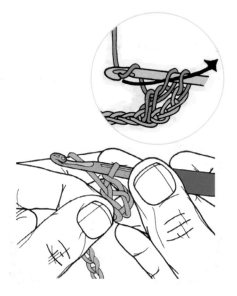

④ Take the yarn over the hook again and pull it back through the last two loops to give one new loop on the hook. Repeat steps 1 to 4 to the end of the row, working into each chain stitch on the foundation chain.

⑤ At the end of the row, turn your work and make three turning chains. On all rows after the first one, make treble crochets into the trebles on the previous row in the same way as in steps 1 to 4, but missing the first treble and sliding the hook under both loops at the top of each stitch (the 'v' shape described on page 20). At the end of the row, work the last treble into the top of the turning chain.

HALF TREBLE (htr)

The name of this stitch describes it well – it's a slightly shorter version of the treble.

① At the beginning of the row, first add a turning chain of two extra chain stitches. Take the working yarn over the hook. Then slide the hook into the third chain stitch on the foundation chain. Pull the yarn back through the first loop on the hook. You should now have three loops on your needle.

2 Take the yarn over the hook again and pull the yarn through all three loops to give one new loop on the hook. Repeat steps 1 to 2 to the end of the row, working into each next chain stitch on the foundation chain.

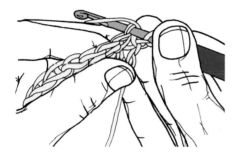

3 At the end of the row, turn your work and make two turning chains. On all rows after the first one, make half treble crochets into the half trebles on the previous row in the same way as in steps 1 to 2, but missing the first half treble and sliding the hook under both loops at the top of each stitch (the 'v' shaped described on page 20). At the end of the row, work the last half treble into the top of the turning chain.

DOUBLE TREBLE (dtr)

This is a slightly taller stitch than the treble and gives you a very open fabric.

1 At the beginning of the row, first add a turning chain of four extra stitches. Take the working yarn over the hook, twice. Then slide the hook into the fifth chain from the hook on the foundation chain. Take the yarn over the hook again, just once. ➤

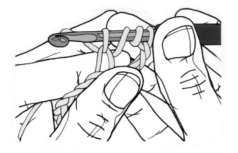

2 Pull the crochet hook through the first loop on the hook. You will now have four loops on the hook.

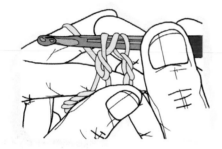

3 Now take the yarn over the hook again and pull it back through the first two loops on the hook. You will now have three loops left on the hook.

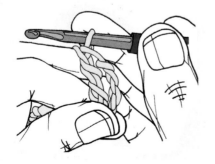

4 Repeat step 3, pulling the yarn through the next two loops on the hook. Repeat again and pull the

RACHEL'S & SARAH'S TIP:
Have a go at making even taller stitches – a triple treble crochet and a quadruple treble crochet – by increasing the number of times you wind the yarn over the hook before starting the stitch and by increasing the number of times you pull the yarn through the loops. Remember, each time you increase the stitch height, you need to add an extra turning chain at the beginning of the row.

yarn through the last two loops to give one remaining loop. Repeat steps 1 to 4 to the end of the row, working into each next chain stitch on the foundation row.

5 At the end of the row, turn your work and make four turning chains. On all rows after the first one, make double treble crochets into the double trebles on the previous row in the same way as in steps 1 to 4, but missing the first double treble and sliding the hook under both loops at the top of each stitch (the 'v' shape described on page 20). At the end of the row, work the last double treble into the top of the turning chain.

next steps

Now that you can do the basic stitches, you're ready to learn some more techniques before you tackle a project.

JOINING IN NEW YARN

Always make sure you have enough yarn to crochet to the end of the row. But don't panic – if you run out, there's a way of joining new working yarn into your fabric.

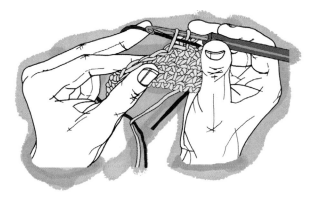 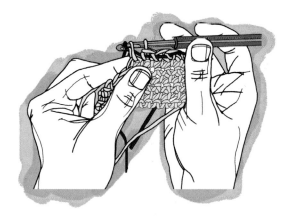

1 Start to work in the end of the new yarn a few stitches before you finish the old yarn. Do this by laying it along the top of the previous row so that you work over it as you make the next few stitches.

2 When you need to change yarns, draw the first loops for the next stitch through with the old yarn. Then pick up the new yarn and draw it through to make the last loop of the stitch. Continue with the new yarn, working over the end of the old yarn to secure it. Neatly snip off the two ends of yarn.

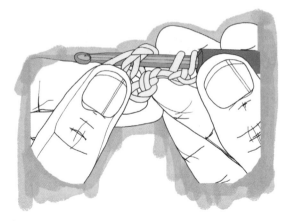

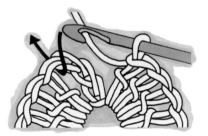

2 To work the stitches for the first round, always insert the hook through the middle of the base ring to draw through the first loop.

3 To finish the first round, insert the hook through the top of the starting chain and work a slip stitch.

RACHEL'S & SARAH'S TIP:
Use a crochet marker to keep track of where you began each round. Every time you begin a round, place a coloured marker on top of your starting chain. If you do not add a marker, it can be easy to confuse which round you are working on, and you may end up adding or losing stitches.

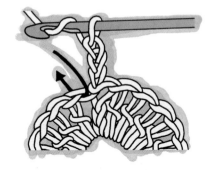

4 For the second round, make a starting chain as usual. Make the stitches on this and all following rounds by inserting the hook under both loops at the top of each stitch on the previous round. Complete the round with a slip stitch.

To keep your crocheted fabric flat, you will need to work two stitches into each stitch on the previous round, increasing (see also page 39) the total number of stitches in each round.

easy decorative stitches

Once you have mastered all the basic stitches, there are lots of ways of working them to create a variety of textures, patterns and shapes. They will give your fabric interest as well as forming the basis for making edgings, buttonholes and fancy motifs.

This sample was worked in double crochet.

WORKING BETWEEN STITCHES

You can work in this way with any type of stitch to create a very firm fabric. The taller the stitch, the easier it will be to manoeuvre the hook.

Insert the hook between two stitches on the previous row, instead of under the top of a stitch. Finish the stitch in the usual way and repeat this way of working across the row.

Always count the stitches after you finish the row to check that you still have the correct number.

Three trebles were worked into each three chain spaces on both samples.

WORKING INTO CHAIN SPACES

If you work into the spaces made by chains along rows or in rounds, you can open up the spaces to create interesting patterns. You can use this method in lots of ways, including making buttonholes, motifs and edgings.

Insert the hook underneath the whole chain on the previous row and then complete working the new stitch in the usual way. Work the number of stitches into one chain space as directed by the pattern.

2dc, 3tr, 2dc worked into each five chain spaces in this sample.

An attractive variation for an edging is to change the stitches worked into the chain space. For example, begin with double crochet, increasing to trebles in the middle and then returning to double crochet.

FRONT AND BACK LOOP CROCHET

Working into the front or the back of stitches produces slightly different effects, but both with distinctive horizontal bars across the fabric.

To work into the front of the loop, simply insert the hook upwards under just the front loop of the stitch on the previous row. Complete the new stitch in the usual way.

To work into the back of the loop, simply insert the hook downwards under just the back loop of the stitch on the previous row. Complete the new stitch in the usual way.

Try experimenting with both these techniques to create more interesting fabrics.

This sample was made by working into the front loops on every row.

This sample was made with alternating rows of front and back crochet.

CROSSED STITCHES

There are several ways of creating crossed stitches. You can cross pairs of short or tall stitches, but the taller the stitch, the clearer the crossed shape.

Make a foundation chain with an even number of chain stitches and then work a turning chain to suit your chosen stitch. Miss one stitch in the previous row and work the new stitch into the next stitch on the previous row. Then work the second new stitch into the missed stitch on the previous row. Repeat this pattern across the row.

This sample has been worked by crossing single treble crochets.

fun textured variations

When you start designing your own crocheted accessories or garments there are many decorative effects you can create just using the basic stitches.

This sample was crocheted in DK yarn with a 4.5mm hook. See pattern below right.

popcorn stitch

Popcorns are groups of complete stitches worked into the same stitch and then closed together at the top to create a very textured fabric. They are often worked in treble, and half or double treble crochet.

HOW TO MAKE A POPCORN

This method is for a three-stitch popcorn, but you can also make popcorns with more or fewer stitches.

Work three treble stitches into the same stitch on the previous row. Remove the hook from the working loop and insert it under both loops at the top of the first treble. Insert the hook back into the working loop and pull it through the other loops on the hook to close the popcorn.

TRY THIS POPCORN PATTERN

Foundation chain: ch a number of sts divisible by 3 plus 2.
Foundation row: 1ch, work in dc across row.
Row 1: 3ch, 1tr, * work popcorn, 2tr*.
Row 2: 1ch, dc across row.
Continue, repeating both these 2 rows.
Fasten off.

bobbles

Each bobble is a cluster of incomplete stitches worked into the same stitch. They are often worked in treble crochet, with shorter stitches on each side to enhance the bumpy effect on the bobbles.

HOW TO MAKE BOBBLE (MB)

This method is for a five-stitch bobble, but you can also make bobbles with more or fewer stitches.

Work five treble stitches into the same stitch on the previous row, but leave the last loop of each one on the hook. You should have six loops on the hook.

Take the yarn over the hook again and draw it through all six loops on the hook, ready to progress to the next stitch.

This sample was crocheted in DK yarn with a 4.5mm hook. See pattern below left.

TRY THIS BOBBLE PATTERN

Foundation chain: ch a number of sts divisible by 4 plus 3 extra.
Foundation row and first two rows: 1ch, work in dc across row.
Row 3: 3ch, 2tr, *MB, 3tr* rep across row.
Rows 4–6: 1ch, work in dc across row.
Row 7: 3ch, *MB, 3tr*, to last two sts, MB, 1tr, rep across row.
Row 8–10: 1ch, work in dc across row.
Repeat rows 3–6 once more.
Fasten off.

bobble bag

My flatmate is forever saying I need a bag for all the yarn and equipment strewn around our flat, so I came up with this gorgeous solution. Of course, it's not only great to keep your crochet stuff in order, it's big and sturdy enough to tote around as a day bag.

MATERIALS   Rowan Big Wool, 2 x 100g balls. I used Sugar Spun. Oddment of chunky yarn in contrast shade.
1 x pair of straight bamboo or wooden handles.

HOOK   12mm

TENSION   6 stitches and 6½ rows to 10cm/4in square over double crochet.

ABBREVIATION

MB: Work 4 complete tr into same stitch (i.e. leaving last loop of each tr on hook), yarn round hook and pull through all 5 loops to make 1 st.

PATTERN

Back
Make 18ch.
Foundation row (WS): 1dc into 2nd ch from hook, 1dc into each ch. 17dc.
Rows 1 and 2: 1ch, 1dc into each dc.
Row 3: 1ch, 2dc, MB, 5dc, MB, 5dc, MB, 2dc.
Rows 4 and 5: 1ch, dc2tog, dc to end. 15dc.
Row 6: 1ch, 1dc into each dc.
Row 7: 1ch, 4dc, MB, 5dc, MB, 4dc.
Rows 8 and 9: 1ch, dc2tog, dc to end. 13dc.
Row 10: 1ch, 1dc into each dc.
Row 11: 1ch, 1dc, MB, 4dc, MB, 4dc, MB, 1dc.
Rows 12 and 13: 1ch, dc2tog, dc to end. 11dc.
Rows 14 and 15: 1ch, 1dc into each dc.
Fasten off. Work front to match.

soft sequined scarf

Who said crochet isn't glamorous? Make this elegant scarf and glam it up with loads of sparkly sequins.

MATERIALS Rowan Kidsilk Haze, 2 x 25g balls in different shades. I used Candy Girl (A) and Splendour (B), Assorted sequins.

HOOK 4.5 mm

TENSION Small circle 7.5cm/3in diameter. Large circle 13cm/5in diameter.

PATTERN

Small circle (make 12)
Use shade A double.

Make 4ch, ss into first ch to form a ring.
Round 1: 3ch, 2tr into ring, 3ch [3tr into ring, 3ch] 4 times, ss into top of 3ch.
Round 2: Ss into each of 2tr, ss into ch sp, 3ch, 2tr into same sp as ss, 3ch [3tr into next ch sp, 3ch], 4 times, ss into top of 3ch.
Fasten off.

Large Circle (make 7)
Use shade B double.

Make 4ch, ss into first ch to form a ring.
Round 1: 3ch, 2tr into ring, 3ch, [3tr into ring, 3ch] 4 times, ss into top of 3ch.
Round 2: Ss into each of the 2tr, ss into ch sp, [3ch, 2tr, 3ch, 3tr, 3ch] all into same sp as ss, [3tr, 3ch] twice into each ch sp, ss into top of 3ch.
Round 3: Ss into each of 2tr, ss into ch sp, 3ch, 2tr into same as ss, 1ch, *[3tr, 1ch] twice into next ch sp, [3tr, 1ch] into next ch sp; rep from * 3 times, [3tr, 1ch] twice into last ch sp, ss into top of 3ch.
Round 4: Ss into each of 2tr, ss into ch sp, 3ch, 2tr into same sp as ss, 1ch, [3tr, 1ch] into each ch sp, ss into top of 3ch. Fasten off.

MAKING UP

Sew a pair of small circles between each large circle, as shown. Sew some sequins in the centre of each circle.

beaded bracelet

Making jewellery with beads and yarn is not nearly as fiddly as you might expect. It's really quite easy, and there are loads of creative possibilities by combining colours, textures and beads.

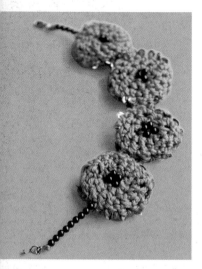

MATERIALS Rowan Cotton Glace, 1 x 50g ball.
I used Maritime.
Beads or sequins.
Clasp fasteners.
Small piece of felt.

HOOK 3.5mm

PATTERN

Bobbles (make 4)
Thread 64 beads or sequins onto yarn.
3ch, ss into first ch to form a ring.
Round 1 (WS): 1ch, 8dc into ring, ss into first dc.
Round 2: 1ch, 2dc into each dc, ss into first dc. 16dc.

Rounds 3 and 4: 1ch, [slide 1 bead up and work 1dc into next dc] to end, ss in first dc.
Round 5: 1ch, [1dc into next dc, miss next dc] to end. 8dc.
Round 6: As round 5. 4dc.
Fasten off.

MAKING UP

Sew up the bobbles, push through the beads or sequins and flatten.
Sew a sprinkling of beads in the centre of each bobble.
Cut 4 felt circles and sew one to the back of each bobble.
Cut a 40cm/16in length of yarn. Attach one half of the fastener securely to the end of yarn, thread on 6–10 beads followed by the 4 bobbles, another 6–10 beads then the other half of the fastener.
Fasten off securely.

wire necklace & earrings

You can also use crocheting techniques to make jewellery from beads and wire. This project uses basic techniques, plus it's a great way to create some cheap but funky jewellery pieces.

MATERIALS Coloured wire from Scientific wire company, www.wires.co.uk.
1 pack of Jaeger beads.
Necklace fastener.
2 earring hooks.

HOOK 4.5mm

PATTERN

Necklace
Circle with beaded edge (make 4):
Make 5ch.
Foundation row: 1dc into 2nd ch from hook, 1dc into each ch. 4dc.
Row 1: 1ch, 1dc into each dc.
Rows 2–15: As row 1.
Fasten off.

Squash to form a small circle. Using a length of wire join 18–20 beads around the edge of the circle, weaving the wire in and out of the circle to secure.

Wire beaded circle (make 3):
Thread 25 beads on the working wire.
Make 6ch.
Foundation row: Push bead up to last ch, 1dc into 2nd ch from hook, [push bead up to last dc, 1dc into next ch] to end. 5dc.
Row 1: 1ch, [push bead up, 1dc into next dc] to end.
Rows 2–4: As row 1.
Fasten off. Mould each wire piece into a circular shape.

End piece (make 2):
Thread 14 beads on working wire.
Make 3ch.
Foundation row: Push bead up to last ch, 1dc in 2nd ch from hook, push bead up to last dc, 1dc in next ch. 2dc.
Row 1: 1ch [push bead up, 1dc in next dc] twice.
Rows 2–6: As row 1.
Fasten off

Earrings
Make 2 circles with beaded edge, as given for necklace.

MAKING UP

For the necklace, secure one half of the fastener onto a length of wire, then weave the wire in and out through one end piece, [across one small circle with beaded edge then across one wire beaded circle] 3 times, across the last small circle with beaded edge, then other end piece. Adjust the length of wire to fit your neck, then secure the other end of fastener in place.

For the earrings, using a small length of wire attach the earring hooks to small circles.

THINGS TO DO WITH YARN:
#1 TIE YOUR HAIR BACK WITH IT

jewellery bags

These beautiful, delicate little bags are ideal for jewellery, make-up or as a very special gift bag for your mum or a close pal.

MATERIALS Rowan Kidsilk Haze, 1 x 25g ball. I used 1 x 25g ball each of Midnight and Hurricane. 50cm x 2cm wide ribbon.

HOOK 5mm

TENSION 11 stitches and 8 rows to 10cm/4in square.

ABBREVIATION

MB: Work 3 incomplete tr into same st (i.e. leaving last loop of each tr on hook), yarn round hook and pull through all 4 loops to make 1 st.

PATTERN

Main part
Using yarn double, make 30ch.
Foundation row: 1dc into 2nd ch from hook, 1dc into each ch. 29dc.

Row 1: 1ch, 1dc into each dc.
Row 2 (RS): 3ch, 1tr into next dc, [MB, 1tr into each of next 2dc] to end.
Rep rows 1 and 2, 5 times, then work row 1 again.
Next row: 4ch, miss first dc, 1dtr into each dc.
Work 3 rows dc.
Fasten off.

Base
Make 4ch, ss into first ch to form a ring.
Round 1: 3ch, 7tr into ring, ss into top of 3ch.
Round 2: 3ch, 1tr into same place as ss, 2tr into each tr, ss into top of 3ch.
Round 3: 1ch, 2dc into each st, ss into first dc.
Fasten off.

MAKING UP

Join the row ends of the main part. With WS together, sew the base to the main part. Weave the ribbon in and out of dtr row on the main part and tie in a bow.

guy's tie

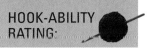

This was an idea I came up with for my friend's band – stripey ties that they could wear at their gigs. Using denim yarn gives this design a modern twist and works day and night.

MATERIALS Rowan Denim, 2 x 50g balls in different shades. I used Memphis (A) and Nashville (B).

HOOK 4.5 mm

TENSION 12 stitches and 12 rows to 10cm/4in square over double crochet, using yarn double.

PATTERN

Use yarn double. With A, make 8ch.
Foundation row: 1dc into 2nd ch from hook, 1dc into each ch. 7dc.
Dc row: 1ch, 1dc into each dc.
Work in dc for 37cm occasionally changing colour to make a stripey fabric.
Next row: 1ch, dc2tog, dc to end of row.
Next row: 1ch, dc2tog, dc to end of row. 5dc.
Work a further 90cm in dc.
Fasten off.

MAKING UP

You will need to line the finished tie with some thick fabric to stop it from twisting and give it firm support. Don't forget, denim yarn decreases in size when washed!

hat & glove set

Cheer yourself up over the winter months with this adorable hat and glove set. Who wouldn't want to brave the short days looking this cute?

MATERIALS Rowan Country, 2 x 50g balls in different shades. I used Clover (A) and Rose (B).

HOOK 9mm

TENSION 8 stitches to 10cm/4in.

PATTERN

Hat
Using A, make 6ch, ss into first ch to form a ring.
Round 1: 3ch, 9tr into ring, ss into top of 3ch.
Round 2: 3ch, working into back loop only work 1tr into same place as ss, 2tr into each tr, ss into top of 3ch. 20sts.
Round 3: As round 2. 40sts.
Rounds 4 and 5: 1ch, working into both loops work 1dc into each st, ss into first dc.
Round 6: Change to B. 1ch, 1dc around stem of each dc, ss into first dc.

Round 7: As round 4.
Round 8: Change to A. work as round 6.
Round 9: As round 4.
Rounds 10 and 11: As rounds 6 and 7.
Round 12: Change to A, 1ch, 1dc into top of each dc, ss into first dc.
Round 13: 1ch, *miss first dc, dc into next 2dc* Rep to end, miss last st, ss into first dc.
Fasten off.

Flower
Using A, make 5ch, ss into first ch to form a ring.
Round 1 (WS): 1ch, 7dc into ring, ss into first dc.
Round 2: [5ch, ss into next dc] 7 times.
Fasten off.
For centre make 4ch using B, ss into first ch to form a ring.
Round 1 (RS): 1ch, 5dc into ring, ss into first dc.
Fasten off. Sew in the centre of flower. Sew the flower onto the side of hat.

Gloves

Using A, make 17ch.

Foundation row (RS): 1dc into 2nd ch from hook, 1dc into each ch. 16dc.

Row 1: 1ch, 1dc into each dc.

Row 2: Change to B, 1ch, 1dc around stem of each dc.

Row 3: 1ch, 1dc in top of each dc.

Rows 4 and 5: Change to A. Work as rows 2 and 3.

Rows 6 and 7: Change to B. Work as rows 2 and 3.

Rows 8 and 9: Change to A. 1ch, 1dc into top of each dc.

Row 10: 3ch, miss first dc, 1tr into back loop of each dc.

Row 11: Change to B, 3ch, miss first tr, 1tr into back loop of each tr, 1tr into top of 3ch.
Fasten off.

Flower (make 2)

Using A, make 3ch, ss into first ch to form a ring.

Round 1 (WS): 1ch, 5dc into ring, ss into first dc.

Round 2: [3ch, ss into next dc] 5 times.
Fasten off.

For centre make 3ch using B, ss into first ch to form a ring.

Round 1: 1ch, 4dc into ring, ss into first dc.
Fasten off.

Join the seam of each glove and use a space between the stitches on the tenth row for the thumb hole. Sew the centre onto the middle of each flower, then sew a flower onto the back of each glove.

THINGS TO DO WITH YOUR CROCHET HOOK:

#2 STIR YOUR TEA WITH IT

geometric scarf

My boyfriend wanted a scarf with a difference, so I came up with this contemporary design. Of course, it would be great for a girl as well. It's simply made up of double squares crocheted together, so you can make it as long as you like by adding more squares. Easy!

MATERIALS Rowan Big Wool, 3 x 100g balls in different shades. I used Best Brown (A), Smoky (B) and Sandstone (C).

HOOK 12mm

TENSION 6 stitches and 7 rows to 10cm/4in square over double crochet.

PATTERN

Using A, make 11ch.
Foundation row: 1dc into 2nd ch from hook, 1dc into each ch. 10dc.
Rows 1–3: Using A, 1ch, 1dc into each dc.
Rows 4–7: Using B, 1ch, 1dc into each dc.
Rows 8–11: Using C, 1ch, 1dc into each dc.
Fasten off.

Make 9 more squares.

MAKING UP

Place the squares in whatever order you like, horizontal or vertical, alternating them to create your own design. Sew up using the woven seam method (see page 37).

shoulder bag

Great for a guy or a girl. This bag has a contemporary, utilitarian design, and is big enough to fit your work books and newspapers.

MATERIALS Rowan Big Wool, 3 x 100g balls in shade A and 2 x 100g balls in shade B. I used Blue Velvet (A) and Smudge (B).

HOOK 15mm

TENSION 5½ stitches and 6½ rows to 10cm/4in square over double crochet.

PATTERN

Back
Using A, make 2ch.
Foundation row: 3dc into 2nd ch from hook.
Begin increase pattern.
Row 1: 1ch, 2dc into first dc, 1dc into next dc, 2dc into last dc. 5dc.
Rows 2–4: 1ch, 2dc into first dc, 1dc into each dc to last dc, 2dc into last dc. 11dc.
Row 5: 1ch, 1dc into each dc.
Rep rows 2–5 once. 17dc.
Break off A.
Join in B, rep rows 2–5 once. 23dc.

Break off B.
Join in A.
Begin decrease pattern.
Next 10 rows: 1ch, miss first dc, 1dc into each dc to last 2dc, miss 1dc, 1dc into last dc. 3dc.
Fasten off.

Front
Work as back.

Strap and gusset
The strap and gusset for this bag are crocheted all in one.
Using B, make 5ch.
Foundation row: 1dc in 2nd ch from hook, 1dc in each of next 3ch. 4dc.
Next row: 1ch, 1dc in each dc.
Continue until strip fits around 3 sides and is long enough to go over shoulder. Fasten off.

MAKING UP

Join the ends of the strap and gusset and sew to 3 sides of the front and back using the woven seam method, leaving the remainder for the shoulder strap.

crocheting
for an occasion

By now, you've probably noticed that a whole world of crochet opportunities has opened up. I've designed these projects with both fun and function in mind. They will give you the confidence to experiment with a fabulous range of yarns and develop techniques including beading, felting, colour-work and even creating your own works of art.

Sarah

tablemat & coasters

These are practical AND stylish. If you're a tableware afficionado, match the colours to your china for the ultimate in dinner party style. If you're not, choose colours that will go with everything and keep your precious tabletops protected!

MATERIALS

Rowan Damask, 1 x 50g ball, used double throughout.
I used Pigment (A).
Rowan Bamboo Tape, 1 x 50g ball. I used Wafer (B).
Rowan 4 ply Cotton, 1 x 50g ball. Used double throughout.
I used Bloom (C).

HOOKS

4mm and 5mm

TENSION

13 stitches and 10 rows to 10cm/4in over htr.

PATTERN

Tablemat
Using 5mm hook and A, make 27ch.
Foundation row: 1htr into second ch from hook, 1htr into each ch.
Row 1: 1ch, 1htr into each htr.
Rep row 1 until you have made a square.
Fasten off.
With RS facing and using C, work a dc edging around square, working extra stitches into the corners, ss into first dc. Work 1 round in B and then C. Fasten off.

Large motifs
Make 1 each in A, B and C.
Round 1: Using 4mm hook, make 4ch, work 13tr into fourth ch from hook, ss into top ch. 14 sts.

Round 2: 3ch, 1tr into same place as ss, [1tr into next tr, 2tr into next tr] 6 times, 1tr into next tr, ss into top of 3ch.
Fasten off.

Small
Make 1 each in A and C.
Using 4mm hook work Round 1 as large motif.
Fasten off.

To finish
Press. Using the photograph on page 76 as a guide, sew the motifs to the mat.

Coaster
Using 5mm hook and A, make 12ch.
Work as tablemat on 11htr.

Motifs
Work 1 large motif each in A and C, but begin round 2 with 1ch, then work dc instead of tr.
Work 1 small motif in B.

To finish
As for tablemats.

THINGS TO DO WITH YARN: #2 TIE YOUR ASPARAGUS

felted oven gloves

These oven gloves will ensure you remain safe yet stylish in even the most heated of situations. Be warned though, they're not suitable for use in or around a naked flame, but they are great for handling hot pots and pans. This design allows you to try a new technique: felting.

MATERIALS   Rowan Country, 4 x 50g balls.
I used Willow (A).
Rowan Big Wool, 1 x 50g ball.
I used Ginger Snap (B).

HOOK   8mm

TENSION   Don't worry too much about tension, as this will alter when the gloves are felted.

PATTERN

Main strip
Using A, make 16ch.
Foundation row: 1dc into 2nd ch from hook, 1dc into each ch. 15dc.
Row 1: 1ch, 1dc into back of loop of each dc.
Continue in pattern as set in Row 1 and at the same time inc 1 st at each end of next and following alternate rows until there are 23 sts.*
Work a further 68 rows in pattern.
Dec 1 st at each end of next row and following alternate rows until 15 sts remain.
Work 2 rows. Fasten off.

Pads (make 2)
Using A, work as main strip to *.
Work a further 14 rows.
Fasten off.

To finish
With the RSs together, sew the pads to the corresponding position of the main strip using backstitch. Turn right side out.

Place in an old pillowcase and wash at 60°C along with a couple of towels to balance the load (see page 44).

Once felted, pull into shape and allow to dry flat. When completely dry, use a large knitter's needle and yarn B to embellish with blanket stitch. Secure first stitch at one edge of the oven glove and then work from left to right. Insert the needle close to the edge, bring back out over the thread loop and pull taut. Continue working evenly spaced stitches in this way along the edge of the oven glove, taking care to only work through one layer of each mitt.

cafetière cover & mug warmers

I came up with this cute design to keep my coffee piping hot and make hot mugs easy to handle. When your friends pop over for coffee they'll love the individual style.

MATERIALS

Rowan Calmer, 3 x 50g ball in different shades. I used Coffee Bean (A), Delight (B) and Calm (C). Rowan buttons: 3 x 00354, 4 x 00380.

HOOK

5mm

TENSION

17 stitches and 22 rows to10cm/ 4in over dc.

ABBREVIATIONS

SP: Work 1dc into next dc 2 rows below.

PATTERN

Cafetière cover
Using A, make 49ch.
Foundation row (RS): 1dc into 2nd ch from hook, 1dc into each ch. 48dc.
Row 1: 1ch, 1dc into each dc.
Rows 2–3: as row 1, changing to B during last dc of row 3.
Row 4: 1ch, [3dc, 2SP]; to last 3dc, 1dc into each dc.
Row 5: As row 1, changing to A during last dc.
Rows 6–7: As row 1, changing to C during last dc of row 7.
Row 8: 1ch, 2dc, [2SP, 3dc] to last dc, 1dc in last dc.
Row 9: As row 1, changing to A during last dc.
Rows 10–11: As row 1, changing to B at end of row 11.
Row 12: 1ch, 1dc, [2SP, 3dc], to last 2dc, 2SP.
Row 13: As row 1, changing to A during last dc.
Rows 14–25: As row 1, changing to B at end of row 25.
Rows 26–27: As rows 4–5.
Rows 28–29: As row 1. Fasten off.

Button band

With RS facing and C, work 25dc evenly along the left edge. Work 6 rows dc. Fasten off.

Buttonhole band

With RS facing and C, work 25dc evenly along right edge.

Work 3 rows dc.

Buttonhole row: 1ch, 1dc into next 3dc, [3ch, miss next 3dc, 1dc into next 5dc] twice, 3ch, miss next 3dc. 1dc into last 3dc.

Next row: 1ch, 1dc into each dc and 3dc into each ch sp. Work 2 rows dc. Fasten off.

Using B, work 1ss around stem of each dc of last row. Fasten off.

Press. Sew on larger buttons.

Mug warmer (make 2)

Using B, make 39ch.

Work as cafetière cover to end of row 3, changing to A during last dc of row 3.

Row 4: As for cafetière cover.

Row 5: As row 1, changing to B during last dc.

Rows 6–9: As row 1.

Fasten off.

Buttonhole band

With RS facing and C, work 9dc evenly along left edge.

Work 3 rows dc.

Buttonhole row: 1ch, 1dc into next 2dc, 1ch, miss 1dc, 3dc, 1ch, miss 1dc, 1dc into last 2dc.

Next row: 1ch, 1dc into each dc and ch sp.

Work 1 row dc. Fasten off.

Using A, work 1ss around stem of each dc of last row. Fasten off.

Press. Sew on smaller buttons.

THINGS TO DO WITH YOUR
CROCHET HOOK:
#3 USE IT AS A BOOKMARK

beaded pencil case

Inspired by all the wonderful stationery on the market, this pencil case is glamorous, yet practical. The combination of beading worked into a closely woven fabric means that none of your vital accessories can escape.

MATERIALS Rowan Handknit Cotton, 1 x 50g. I used Celery (A).
Small amount of Slick (B).
78 x size 6 beads. I used SB2630 (orange/lime).
60 x size 6 beads. I used SB209 (pink/clear).

HOOK 3mm

TENSION 19dc and 22 rows to 10cm/4in.

PATTERN

Thread beads onto yarn alternating 13 orange and 12 pink, until all beads are threaded.

Using A, make 34ch.
Foundation row: 1dc into 2nd ch from hook, 1dc into each ch. 33dc.
Row 1: 1ch, 1dc into each dc.
Row 2: As row 1

Row 3 (WS): 1ch, 1dc into each of next 4dc, [slide bead up and work 1dc into next dc, 1dc into next dc, 1dc into next dc] 13 times, 1dc into each of last 3dc.
Rows 4–6: As row 1.
Row 7: 1ch, 1dc into each of next 5dc, [slide bead up and work 1dc into next dc, 1dc into next dc] 12 times, 1dc into each of the last 4dc.
Rows 8–10: As row 1.
Rep rows 3–10, 4 times, then work rows 3–6 again.
Fasten off.

To finish
Do not press.
With RS facing and using B, work 1ss around the stem of each dc of last row. Fasten off.
Using the photograph as a guide, fold the fabric to form an 'envelope'. With RS facing and using B, join sides by working a row of dc through all thicknesses.
Fasten off.

artwork

The idea behind this artwork is to encourage you to appreciate how far crochet has travelled from its original image. The instructions should be seen as a springboard for you to develop your own ideas. Have fun!

square of circles

MATERIALS Small amounts of Rowan Cotton Glace. I used Butter, Twilight and Damson.
Small amounts of Rowan 4 ply. I used Aegean and Violetta.
Rowan buttons: I used 4 x 00378, 3 x 00347, 2 x 00349.
Canvas block 15cm x 15cm/6in x 6in (available from discount art shops).
Double-sided tape.
9mm x 25mm/⅓in x 1in brass curtain rings.

HOOK 3.5mm

PATTERN

Small circle (make 4)
Use colour combinations of your choice.
Round 1: Work 30dc into curtain ring. Join with a ss.
Change colour.
Round 2: 1ch, 1dc into each dc. Join with a ss.*
Fasten off.

Large circle (make 5)
Use colour combinations of your choice.
Work as small circle to*. Change colour.
Round 3: 1ch, 1dc into same place, [1dc into next dc, 2dc into next dc], to last dc, 1dc into last dc. Join with a ss. Fasten off.

To finish
Press circles.
Attach strips of double-sided tape to the canvas and then arrange the circles according to your taste.
Place the button in the centre of each circle.

wire flowers

MATERIALS   Hand-made paper (or background of choice), measuring 3cm larger than chosen canvas block.
Canvas block as before.
Selection of beads.
Scientific Wire Company (see page 59): 0.200mm silver plated craft wire, coloured craft wire. I used opaque purple.

HOOK   3.5mm

PATTERN

Large flower
Use silver wire double throughout.
Make 5ch, ss in first ch to form a ring.
Round 1: 3ch, 25tr into ring, ss into top of 3ch.
Round 2: 1ch, [3ch, miss next tr, 1dc into next tr] to end, 3ch, ss into first ch. Fasten off.

Medium flower
Make 1 with a single thread of silver wire and one with silver wire used triple throughout.
Make 5ch, ss into first ch to form a ring.
Round 1: 1ch, 15dc into ring, ss into first ch.
Round 2: 1ch, [3ch, miss next dc, 1dc into next dc] to last dc, 3ch, ss into first ch. Fasten off.

Small flower
Make 1 with a single thread of silver wire. Work as medium flower to end of round 1. Fasten off.

Make another in the same way, with a single thread of silver wire and a single thread of opaque purple. For the top layer of this flower, use a single thread of opaque purple and work as medium flower to end of round 1. Fasten off.

To finish
Position the flowers on the paper and thread the loose wires through to the back. This will help to secure them. Stitch the beads into the flowers and through the paper to accent different parts of the flowers. Attach the paper to the canvas to the block using double-sided tape and mitre the corners to achieve a neat edge.

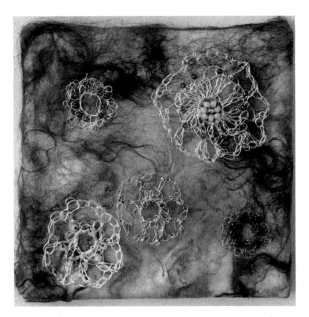

THINGS TO DO
WITH YARN:

#3

HANG TEALIGHTS

cushion cover

Here, I've woven a basic mesh with fabrics to achieve a net-like texture.
Adding fabrics and fibres of your choice will enable you to match it to your
own surroundings.

MATERIALS

Rowan Calmer, 1 x 50g ball.
I used Kiwi.
30cm/12in of Kaffe Fassett
Fabric Collection in Roman
Glass, cut into 2.5cm/1in strips.
I used red and green.
Cushion pad, 30cm/12in square.

HOOK

5mm

TENSION

17 stitches to 10cm/4in.

PATTERN

Front
Make 54ch.
Foundation row: 1tr into 6th chain from the hook,
[1ch, miss 1ch, 1tr into next ch] to end.
Row 1: 4ch, miss first tr [1tr into next tr, 1ch] to
end, 1tr in 2nd of each ch.
Rep row 1 until front is square.
Fasten off.

To finish
Press.
Fold fabric strips in half, (so that pattern is showing)
and weave in and out of the mesh as illustrated or
according to a pattern of your choice. Tucking in any
loose ends as you go, slip stitch the panel onto your
cushion pad. Back with a contrasting fabric or make
another panel to match or contrast.

greeting cards

Individually designed cards are a great way to tell someone you really care about them. You could also get creative and make invitations or thank-you cards.

jolly jacquard (far left)

MATERIALS Small amount of Rowan Cotton Glace. I used Oyster (A), Mocha Choc (C) and Butter (D). Rowan Lurex Shimmer. I used Bronze (B). 1 blank card, approx 15cm/6in square. Double-sided tape.

HOOK 3.5mm

PATTERN

Note – Work last dc before changing colour in this way: insert hook into st, yarn round hook and draw loop through, now change colour and draw new colour through 2 loops on hook. Strand colour not in use loosely across WS of panel.

Crochet panel
Using A, make 16ch.
Foundation row (RS): Using A, 1dc into 2nd ch from hook, 1dc into each of next 2ch [using B, 1dc into each of next 3ch; using A, 1dc into each of next 3ch] twice.

Row 1: Using A, 1ch, 3dc, [3dc in B, 3dc in A] twice.
Row 2 and 3: As row 1.
Rows 4–7: Using C, 1ch, 3dc [3dc in D, 3dc in C] twice.
Rows 8–11: As row 1.
Rep rows 4–11 once.
Fasten off.
Using D, work 1 round of dc evenly around panel, work 2dc into each corner, ss in first dc. Fasten off.

To finish
Press.
Attach 3 strips of double-sided tape to blank card and add crocheted panel.

flower garden

Use a background paper as inspiration for your crocheted greeting. Look out for papers with interesting shapes and colour schemes and let inspiration take over.

MATERIALS Oddments of Rowan Cotton Glace.
I used In the Pink (A) and
Damson (B).
Jaeger Pure Silk DK. I used
Sorbet (C)
Rowan Lurex Shimmer. I used
Claret (D).
Card blank approx 12cm/4³/₄in
square.
Double-sided tape.

HOOK 3.5mm

PATTERN

First circle (from left)
Using A, make 6ch, ss into first ch to form a ring.
Round 1: 3ch, 19tr into the ring, ss into top of 3ch.

Round 2: Fasten off A; join D. 1dc into each tr, ss into first dc. Fasten off.

Second circle
As first circle, using B and C.

Third circle
As first circle, using C and A.

Fourth circle
Using A, make 6ch, ss into first ch to form a ring.
Round 1: 1ch, 10dc into ring, ss into first dc. Fasten off A; join B.
Round 2: 3ch, 1tr into same place as ss, 2tr into each dc, ss into top of 3ch. Fasten off.

To finish
Press.
Cut the background paper to size and attach to the card with double-sided tape.
Run a strip of double-sided tape where the background paper meets the card.
Attach the motifs so that they overlap slightly and form an interesting line.

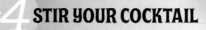

**THINGS TO DO WITH
YOUR CROCHET HOOK:**

#4 STIR YOUR COCKTAIL

hot water bottle cover

This design challenges the rather frumpy image of a hot water bottle cover!
Now you can keep snug without compromising your street cred.

MATERIALS

Rowan Calmer: 1 x 50g.
I used Coral (A).
Small amounts of Kiwi (B) and
Khaki (C).

HOOK

5mm

TENSION

14 htr and 10 rows to 10 cm/4in.

ABBREVIATIONS

Htr2tog: leaving last loop of each st on hook work
1htr into each of next 2 sts, yrh and pull through all
3 loops.

PATTERN

Hot water bottle cover
Using A, make 29ch.
Foundation row: 1dc into 2nd ch from hook,
1dc into each ch. 28dc.
Row 1: 2ch, 1htr into each dc.
Row 2: 2ch, 1htr into each htr.
Rows 3–7: As row 2, changing to B during last st
of row 7.
Row 8: 1ch, 1dc into each htr, changing to C during
last st of row.

Row 9: 1ch, 1dc into each dc, changing to A during
last st of row.
Row 10: 2ch, 1htr into each dc.
Row 11: 2ch, htr2tog, 1htr into each htr to last
2 sts, htr2tog.
Rows 12–13: As row 11. 22 sts.
Row 14: As row 2. Mark each end of last row with
a contrast thread.
Row 15: As row 2.
Row 16: 2ch, 2htr into next htr, 1htr into each htr to
last st, 2htr into last st.
Rows 17–18: As row 16. 28 sts.
Rows 19–33: As row 2.
Row 34: 2ch, [htr2tog] twice, 1htr into each htr to
last 4 sts, [htr2tog] twice.
Row 35: As row 34.
Row 36: 2ch, [htr2tog] 3 times, 1htr into each htr to
last 6 sts, [htr2tog] 3 times. 14 sts.
Rows 37–39: As row 2, changing to B during last st
of row 39.
Row 40: 1ch, 1dc into each htr, changing to C
during last st.
Row 41: 1ch, 1dc into each dc, changing to A
during last st of row.
Row 42: As row 1.
Row 43: As row 16. 16 sts.
Rows 44–45: As row 2. Mark each end of last row
with a contrast thread.

handy bottle bag

We all know how important it is to carry water with us, especially on hot days. Now you can keep your hands free and avoid bulging handbags with this fun and practical bottle carrier.

MATERIALS   Rowan Denim, 1 x 50g ball. I used Tennessee (A) and Nashville (B).

HOOK   4mm

TENSION   19 stitches and 22 rows to 10cm/4in measured over dc.

PATTERN

Bottle carrier:
Using A, make 4ch.
Round 1: 11tr into fourth ch from hook, ss into top ch. 12 sts.
Round 2: 3ch, 1tr into same place as ss, 2tr into each tr, ss into top of 3ch. 24 sts.
Round 3: As round 2. 48 sts.
Round 4: 1ch, 1dc into same place as ss, 1dc into each tr, ss into first dc.
Round 5: 1ch, 1dc into each dc, ss into first dc.
Rounds 6 and 7: As round 5.
Rounds 8 and 9: Using B, as round 5.
Rounds 10–12: using A, as round 5.
Round 13: 1ch, 1dc into same place as ss, 3ch, miss 3dc [1dc into next dc, 3ch, miss 3dc] to end, ss into first dc.

Round 14: 1ch, 1dc into same place as ss, 3ch, [1dc into dc, 3ch] to end, ss into first dc.
Rounds 15–30: As round 14.
Round 31: 1ch, 1dc into each dc and 3dc into each ch sp, ss into first dc. 48 sts.
Work 4 rounds dc in A, 2 rounds in B and 3 rounds in A.
Fasten off.

Strap
Using A, make a 140cm/55in length of ch.
Foundation row (WS): 1htr into 3rd ch from hook, 1htr into each ch.
Edging (RS): With RS of foundation row facing and using B, work 1dc into each st of last row, then 1dc into each of foundation ch. Fasten off.

To finish
Press.
Find the midpoint of the strap and slip stitch into place across the base of carrier. Thread each remaining length through the bars at opposite sides of the mesh and slip stitch into place up the sides of the carrier until you reach the top. Place one strap end underneath the other in order to achieve the desired length and slip stitch into place.

THINGS TO DO WITH YARN:
#4 TIE A BUNCH OF FLOWERS

rag rug

Inspired by the idea of making rugs from rags, this version uses a luxury silk/cotton yarn while retaining a sense of simplicity. This rug would look great in a bathroom or at the entrance to your beach hut! My tension is only a guide; it really doesn't matter if your rug is bigger or smaller.

MATERIALS Rowan Summer Tweed: 2 x 50g hanks in four shades. I used Cotton Bud (white), Dew (lime), Sprig (green) and Powder (blue). Beads (optional). I used some from the KYLAS3/T selection from Beads and Perles.

HOOK 8mm

The rug is worked in three panels, joined and trimmed with double crochet and decorated with shell buttons.

TENSION 9dc and 10 rows to 10cm, using yarn double.

PATTERN

Panel 1
Use yarn double throughout.
Using lime, make 19ch.
Foundation row (WS): 1dc into 2nd ch from hook, 1dc into each ch. 18dc.
Row 1: 1ch, 1dc into each dc.
Continue in dc stripes: 1 row green • 3 rows blue • 1 row white • 1 row lime 1 row blue • 3 rows green • 3 rows white 1 row lime • 2 rows green • 2 rows blue 1 row white • 4 rows green • 1 row lime 1 row blue • 5 rows green • 1 row blue 3 rows white • 1 row lime • 2 rows blue 2 rows green • 1 row lime • 1 row blue 1 row white. Fasten off.

Panel 2
Using yarn double throughout. Using blue, make 19ch. Work as Panel 1 but using the following stripe sequence:
3 rows blue • 3 rows lime • 1 row white 2 rows blue • 2 rows green • 1 row lime 4 rows blue • 1 row white • 1 row green 5 rows blue • 1 row green • 3 rows lime

1 row white • 2 rows green • 2 rows blue
1 row white • 1 row green • 1 row lime
2 rows white • 1 row blue • 3 rows green
1 row lime • 1 row white • 1 row green
Fasten off.

Panel 3

Use yarn double throughout. Using lime, make
19ch. Work as Panel 1 but using the following stripe
sequence:
4 rows lime • 1 row blue • 1 row green
5 rows lime • 1 row green • 3 rows white
1 row blue • 2 rows green • 2 rows lime
1 row blue • 1 row green • 1 row white
2 rows blue • 1 row lime • 3 rows green
1 row white • 1 row blue • 1 row green
3 rows lime • 3 rows green • 1 row blue
2 rows lime • 2 rows green • 1 row white
Fasten off.

To Finish

Press. Use yarn double throughout. With RS
facing and using white, work 2 rows dc along the
row ends of left-hand edge of panel 2. With RSs
together and using white, join panel 3 to the edging
of panel 2 working a row of dc through both panels.
Fasten off.

With RS facing and using white, work 2 rows dc
along the row ends of right-hand edge of panel 1.
Join the edging of panel 1 to the lower edges of
panels 2 and 3. Fasten off.

With RS facing and using white, work 1 round dc
around the outer edge, working 3dc into each
corner, ss into first dc. Fasten off.

Using the photograph as a guide, sew on the
buttons by pulling the yarns through to the front
of the buttons and tying off to secure.

THINGS TO DO WITH YOUR CROCHET HOOK:

#5 **USE IT AS A TELEPHONE DIALLER**

customising designs

Recently there seems to be huge interest in recycling and customising clothes. I regularly take scissors to my latest charity buy or old, tired denims and plain tops. Customising is a fast and cost-effective method of making something new and fashionable. Visit your local thrift shop or rummage through your drawers for things that are crying out for a revamp. All you need is a bit of confidence and some creative thinking.

Rachel x

edgings

My edging designs are straightforward and will take no time at all to crochet up. By adding a simple trimming to a garment or accessory you can easily transform something plain into something very decorative. And don't hesitate to experiment with yarn shades.

edging 1

MATERIALS Rowan Little Big Wool, 1 x 50g ball Amber.

HOOK 9mm

PATTERN
Make a multiple of 3ch plus 1 extra.
Row 1: 1dc into 2nd ch from hook, 1dc into each ch.
Row 2: [1ss into dc, 5tr into next dc, 1ss into next dc] to end. Fasten off.

edging 2

MATERIALS Kidsilk Haze, 1 x 25g ball Splendour (A). Kidsilk Night, 1 x 25g ball Oberon (B).

HOOK 4.5mm

PATTERN
Use yarn double throughout.
Using A, make length of ch required for edging.
Row 1: 1dc into 2nd ch from hook, 1dc into each ch.
Row 2: 3ch, miss first dc, 1tr into each dc.
Row 3: 1ch, 1dc into each tr, 1dc into top of 3ch.
Rows 4–5: As rows 2–3.
Row 5: Join B to first dc, 1ss in first dc, [10ch, 1ss in next dc] to end. Fasten off.

edging 3

__MATERIALS__ Rowan Kid Classic, 1 x 50g
ball Crystal.
__HOOK__ 5mm

PATTERN
Thread on your buttons – the number will depend
on the length of edging required.
Make a multiple of 7ch plus 4 extra.
__Row 1:__ 1dc into 2nd ch from hook, 1dc into
each ch.
__Rows 2 and 3:__ 1ch, 1dc into each dc.
__Row 4:__ 1ch, 1dc into first dc, [wrap yarn 8 times
around hook, insert hook in next st, slide button up
to hook, take yarn over hook at left of button and
complete dc then pull hook through all 8 loops, 1dc
into each of next 6dc] to end, ending 1dc into last
dc. Fasten off.

edging 4

__MATERIALS__ Rowan Damask, 1 x 50g ball
Pigment.
__HOOK__ 4.5mm

PATTERN
Make a multiple of 5ch plus 2 extra.
__Row 1:__ 1dc into 2nd ch from hook, 1dc into
each ch.
__Row 2:__ 1ch, 1dc into each dc.
__Row 3:__ 1ss into first dc, [5ch, miss 4dc,
1ss into next dc] to end.
__Row 4:__ 1ch, 7dc into each ch sp.
Fasten off.

edging 5

__MATERIALS__ Rowan Bamboo Tape, 1 x 50g
ball Wode.
__HOOK__ 4.5mm

PATTERN
Thread beads onto yarn before beginning; the
number will depend on length of edging required.
Make a multiple of 3ch, plus 1 extra.
__Rows 1:__ 1dc into 2nd ch from hook, 1dc into
each ch.
__Row 2:__ 1ch, 1dc into each dc.
__Row 3:__ [1ss into dc, 2ch, push bead up to last ch,
2ch, miss 1dc, 1ss into next dc] to end. Fasten off.

girl's casual top

This is a great way to reinvent your clothes when you're a bit short of money. Visit your local thrift shop, pick out a pretty top, have a rummage in your yarn collection for something pretty to match and customise your fabric with a delicate crocheted edging. This is so easy to do and a great way to recycle and use up your oddments of yarn.

MATERIALS   Jaeger Pure Silk DK, 1 x 50g ball.
             I used Slate.

HOOK   3.5mm

PATTERN

Edging
Make a length of ch to fit around lower edge of top, working a multiple of 3ch plus 1 extra.
Work in dc for as many rows as you like. For my border I worked 6 rows in dc before working my lace trim.

Lace trim
Row 1: [Ss into dc, 5ch, ss into 3rd ch from hook (picot), 2ch, miss 1dc, ss into next dc] to last 3 sts, ss into next st, 5ch, ss into 3rd ch from hook, miss next dc, 1tr into last dc.
Row 2: Ss into first picot, [5ch, ss into next picot] to end. Fasten off.

Inset
Make 5ch
Foundation row: 1dc into 2nd chain from hook, 1dc into each ch. 4dc
Row 1: 1ch, 2dc into first dc, 1dc into each dc. Rep row 1 until inset is required size and there is a multiple of 3dc.
Work 2 rows of lace trim as edging. Fasten off.

Making up
To sew on your edging, first pin the edging around the lower edge of the top and using a fine needle and matching sewing thread, sew loosely in place. Sew inset in place.

denim skirt

Everyone loves their denim, but they do tend to look the same. Try adding your own touches to some old denim pieces or high-street basics with this stylish edging.

MATERIALS Rowan Denim, 2 x 50g balls. I used Tennessee.

HOOK 5mm

PATTERN

Edging
Foundation ch: Make a length of ch to fit around hem of skirt, working a multiple of 4 sts plus 2 extra.
Foundation row (RS): 1dc into 2nd ch from hook, 1dc into each ch.
Row 1: 1ch, 1dc into each dc.
Row 2: 1ch, 1dc into first dc, [8ch, miss 3dc, 1dc into next dc] to end.
Row 3: [5dc, 3tr, 3dtr] into each ch sp.

Belt
Make 5ch, ss first ch to form a ring.
Foundation row: 4ch, [4tr, 3ch, 5tr] into ring, turn.
Row 1: 4ch, [4tr, 3ch, 4tr] into 3 ch sp, ss into top of turning chain, turn.
Rep row 1 for required length for belt.

Making up
Sew the edging along the bottom of skirt with matching thread. Weave the belt under the belt loops on the skirt and tie.

girl's bow top

If your summer hols are looming but your clothes funds are running low, then why not try customising one of your plain vests or t-shirts? This is a really feminine way of adding detail to a plain top.

MATERIALS   Rowan Handknit Cotton,
2 x 50g balls.
I used Tennessee.

HOOK   4.5mm

PATTERN

Bow
Bullion stitch: Wrap yarn 8 times around hook, insert hook into next st, yrh and pull loop through then, one at a time, pull through each of the 8 strands of yarn.
Make 13ch.
Foundation row: 1dc into 2nd ch from hook, 1dc into each ch. 12dc.
Rows 1 and 2: 1ch, 1dc into each dc.
Row 3 (RS): 3ch, miss first dc, [1 bullion st into next dc, 1ch, miss 1dc] 5 times, 1tr into last dc.
Rows 4–6: 1ch, 1dc into each st.
Rep rows 3–6, 15 times.
Fasten off.

Knot
Make 7ch.
Foundation row: 1dc into 2nd ch from hook, 1dc into each ch. 6dc.
Row 1: 1ch, 1dc into each dc.
Rep row 1, 16 times.
Fasten off.

Belt
Make 7ch.
Foundation row: 1dc into 2nd ch from hook, 1dc into each ch. 6dc.
Row 1: 1ch, 1dc into each dc.
Rep row 1 until belt fits around vest at waistline.
Fasten off.

Making up
Fold the main fabric to form a bow shape. Wrap the middle around the centre of bow and sew securely in place. Join the ends of the belt. Attach the bow to the belt, then sew the belt onto the vest using matching sewing thread.

recycled handbag

This is so easy to do; all you need is an old jumper, some yarn and a pair of scissors and, voila, your jumper is now a handbag!

MATERIALS Rowan Kid Classic, 2 x 50g balls in different shades. I used Glacier (A) and Shebert Dip (B). Press stud fastener.

HOOK 5mm

DIRECTIONS FOR CUSTOMISING

1. Pull out a jumper you don't wear any more, or find a second-hand one from a charity shop (make sure it is at least 70 per cent wool).

2. First felt the jumper by putting it in the washing machine at 60°C (see page 44). Once dry, cut off the top part and the sleeves.

3. You should now have two rectangular pieces. Mine are 32cm x 26cm/22¹/₂in x 10¹/₄in.
4. Cut up the sleeves to use as the sides and

base of the bag, pin all the pieces together and sew up inside out using a matching colour of sewing thread.

ABBREVIATIONS

MB: Work 6 incomplete tr into same st until you have 7 loops, pull yarn through all 7 loops to make 1 st.

PATTERN

Handles (make 2)
Using A, make 8ch.
Foundation row: 1dc into 2nd ch from hook, 1dc into each ch. 7dc.
Row 1: 1ch, 1dc into each dc.
Row 2: As row 1.
Row 3: 1ch, 1dc into each of 3dc, MB into next st, 1dc into each of 3dc.
Rows 4–6: 1ch, 1dc into each st.

Rep rows 3–6, 11 more times (or more until you have achieved your required length).

Small pompom (make 2)
Using B, make 2ch, 8dc in 2nd ch from hook, [2dc into next dc, 1dc into next dc] 4 times; [2dc into next dc, 1dc into each of next 2dc] 4 times*; work 32 dc; ** [miss 1dc, 1dc into each of next 3dc] 4 times; [miss 1dc, 1dc into each of next 2dc] 4 times. Fasten off leaving a long end. Stuff the pompom with scraps of yarn and then close the hole.

Large pompom (make 1)
Using A, work as small pompom to * [2dc into next dc, 1dc into each of next 3dc] 4 times; work 40dc; [miss 1dc into each of next 4dc] 4 times. Complete as small pompom from **.

Making up
With WSs together, join the handles, stuff with yarn and sew inside the top of bag at each side. Sew the press stud fastener inside the top of the bag. For the drawstring, use 1 strand A and 1 strand B together. Starting at the centre front, thread the yarn in and out through the bag at the base of the rib. Attach the pompoms to the ends of the drawstring.

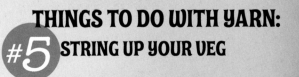

THINGS TO DO WITH YARN:

#5 STRING UP YOUR VEG

girl's elegant top

By adding this simple neckline to a charity shop purchase you can give a plain-looking garment a completely different style. Once felted, it only takes a couple of hours to make.

MATERIALS Rowan Kidsilk Night, 1 x 25g ball.
I used Oberon.
Rowan Kid Classic, 2 x 50g balls.
I used Crystal.
90cm/35½in of 15mm
½in wide satin ribbon.

HOOK 4.5mm

DIRECTIONS FOR CUSTOMISING

Find a long-sleeved, over-sized jumper in a charity shop or use an existing one (make sure it is at least 70 per cent wool).

Felt it by putting it in the washing machine at 60°C (see page 44). Cut the sleeves and neck off.

Pattern for neckline

Using Kidsilk Haze and Kid Classic together make a length of ch to fit around neck.

Row 1 (RS): 1dc into 2nd ch from hook, 1dc into each ch.
Row 2: 1ch, 1dc around stem of each dc.
Rep these 2 rows for the required depth of neckline. Now begin to decrease.
Next row: 1ch, [miss 1dc, 1dc into each of next 2dc] to end.
Next row: 1ch, 1dc around stem of each dc.
Next row: 1ch, [miss 1dc, 1dc into each of next 2dc] to end. Fasten off.

Making up

Join ends using slip stitch method (see page 21) and sew around the neck. Thread ribbon through the top edge, pull tight to pull neckline together and tie in a bow.

index

acknowledgements

We have loved every minute of working on this book. It has been a journey in our world of crafts we will never forget and we would like to say a big thank you to everyone at Kyle Cathie who gave us the chance to work on such a fun project. Our editors, Danielle and Muna, our copy editor, Karen, photographer Kate, illustrator Roberta, designer Jenny and all our gorgeous models!

From Rachel:
I would really like to say a big thank you to Sharon Brant for all her help and encouragement since starting out at Rowan Yarns, and Rein Hilde Van Der Brand for teaching me some of those very cool crochet techniques!

Most of all I would like to thank Sarah for her constant enthusiasm, inspiration and humour while working on the book and not forgetting my parents for continuing to support me throughout my knitting and crocheting journey.

Rachel x

From Sarah:
My first thank you must go to Rachel for inviting me to join her in writing the book – totally cool! A huge thank you to Sharon Brant at Rowan Yarns who got me crocheting in the first place and who never fails to support me and make me laugh! Also to the many fabulous knitters and designers I have met through Rowan – Emma King, Debbie Abrahams, Jane Crowfoot: they never fail to inspire and encourage. A special thank you to Shubhen Chitnis up in Holmfirth for keeping me supplied with yarn. My ability to write the book would not have been possible without the help of friends – Alison, Karen, Vic and Julie; and my amazing family – Simon, mum and dad – the best! My fantastic husband, Paul, and wonderful daughter, Phoebe – so many thanks and even more love!

Dedicated to the memory of my beautiful dog, Merton.

Sarah